INTRO TO
HORSE POLO

BY MARCIA AMIDON LUSTED

SADDLE UP!

SportsZone

An Imprint of Abdo Publishing
abdopublishing.com

abdopublishing.com

Published by Abdo Publishing, a division of ABDO, PO Box 398166, Minneapolis, Minnesota 55439. Copyright © 2018 by Abdo Consulting Group, Inc. International copyrights reserved in all countries. No part of this book may be reproduced in any form without written permission from the publisher. SportsZone™ is a trademark and logo of Abdo Publishing.

Printed in the United States of America, North Mankato, Minnesota
102017
012018

Cover Photo: Shutterstock Images
Interior Photos: Shutterstock Images, 1; Perry Correll/Shutterstock Images, 5, 6; Tim Clayton/Corbis Sport/Getty Images, 8–9; View Stock Stock Connection USA/Newscom, 10–11; DeAgostini/SuperStock, 12; AP Images, 14–15; iStockphoto, 17, 22–23, 24–25, 31, 45; Dean Mouhtaropoulos/Getty Images Sport/Getty Images, 18–19; Dennis W. Donohue/Shutterstock Images, 27; Chris Van Lennep Photo/iStockphoto, 28; Alain Benainous/Gamma-Rapho/Getty Images, 32; Thor Jorgen Udvang/Shutterstock Images, 35; Caro/Frank Sorge/Newscom, 37; James Schwabel/Alamy, 38–39; PA Wire URN:17173712/Press Association/AP Images, 40–41; The polo experience/Alamy, 42–43

Editor: Marie Pearson
Series Designer: Laura Polzin
Content Consultant: Paige Clark, B.S. Equine Science, University of Minnesota Crookston

Publisher's Cataloging-in-Publication Data
Names: Lusted, Marcia Amidon, author.
Title: Intro to horse polo / by Marcia Amidon Lusted.
Description: Minneapolis, Minnesota : Abdo Publishing, 2018. | Series: Saddle up! | Includes online resources and index.
Identifiers: LCCN 2017946918 | ISBN 9781532113413 (lib.bdg.) | ISBN 9781532152290 (ebook)
Subjects: LCSH: Polo--Juvenile literature. | Horsemanship--Juvenile literature. | Horse sports--Juvenile literature.
Classification: DDC 796.353--dc23
LC record available at https://lccn.loc.gov/2017946918

TABLE OF
CONTENTS

CHAPTER 1
A GAME ON HORSEBACK.................... 4

CHAPTER 2
POLO FROM ANCIENT TIMES.................... 10

CHAPTER 3
THE RULES OF THE GAME.......................... 16

CHAPTER 4
THE PLAYERS: HORSE AND RIDER.............. 26

CHAPTER 5
PLAYING POLO AROUND THE WORLD 36

GLOSSARY 46
ONLINE RESOURCES................................. 47
MORE INFORMATION 47
INDEX... 48
ABOUT THE AUTHOR 48

1

A GAME ON HORSEBACK

Eight players on horseback gallop down a field of bright green grass. The field is the size of nine football fields put together. Four players wear red jerseys. Four wear black, blue, and gold. Each player holds a long-handled mallet. As his or her horse moves at full speed down the field, a player leans over and tries to hit a small solid plastic ball. It is approximately 3 inches (7.6 cm) wide and very difficult to hit from the back of a moving horse.

The two teams weave and gallop around the field. The object is to hit the ball through the other team's goal.

Polo is a fast team sport.

Polo players must have good balance to lean over and hit the ball at a gallop.

As the announcer chatters excitedly, describing each team's movements, the black team's Number Two player knocks the ball down the field, passing it to the Number One player on his team. Number One hits the ball toward the red team's goal. There are no goaltenders in polo. The red team's Number Four plays defense and tries to move the ball away from his team's goal. But the black team works together, and with one good hit of his mallet, the Number One black player sends the ball rolling through the red goal. The spectators in the stands yell with approval, and the announcer excitedly calls out the score. The game continues until finally the black team wins, 13 to 11. The players congratulate each other, and their tired horses are led off to be groomed and to rest.

A TEAM SPORT

Just what is this game? It might seem like an odd combination of soccer, football, and horseback riding. It may not be familiar to many Americans. But this game, called polo (or horse polo, to tell it apart from other types of polo), is thousands of years old. It has been played all over the world, from ancient times to the present day. And in some countries, people follow their polo teams with as much energy as any football or basketball fan.

Polo is a game of traditions. Spectators at some polo matches, especially those that take place at polo clubs, dress up in their best clothes. Women wear huge, fancy hats. During the halftime, or between the game's periods,

spectators go out on the field and stomp down the divots of earth and grass that the horses' hooves have churned up. This makes the field smoother again for play.

But polo is also a serious sport. Players must be skilled at both riding and hitting the ball. They must control their horses while also engaging in the game and getting the ball into the goal. Their horses must have stamina for long periods of galloping. They must be able to turn quickly. They must also be well-trained and tuned to the signals and body language of their riders. But for people who love both riding and competitive sports, horse polo can be the perfect game.

Flat shoes are useful for stomping down the grass and soil on the field.

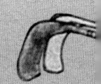

POLO FROM ANCIENT TIMES

Perhaps the first people to play a ball game from horseback were warriors in Central Asia. They played more than 2,000 years ago. They always traveled and had no settled homes, so the game was probably part war training and part fun. As many as 100 warriors played on each team.

Because the first polo players moved from place to place, they spread the game wherever they went. It moved into Persia, then to China, India, and Japan. The first

Polo has been shown in ancient artwork.

During the 1700s, games of polo were played in the Mughal Empire's court in what is now India.

record of a polo tournament was in 600 BCE between the Turkmen and the Persians. The Turkmen won.

Polo was used to train cavalry soldiers during the Middle Ages because the entire game was played on horseback. It was like a miniature battle. Polo spread to Burma, India, and Malta, where British plantation owners learned it. A polo club formed in Kolkata, India, in 1862. It is the oldest polo club in the world. Visiting British army officers learned the sport and brought it back home to England. The first British polo game, which they initially called "hockey on horseback," took place in 1869. It was organized by army officers who had read about the game in a magazine. The first formal written rules for polo were created not long after this first game.

James Gordon Bennett, who watched a polo game during a trip to England in 1875, decided to bring the game back to the United States. He was the publisher of the *New York Herald* newspaper. He came home in 1876 with a copy of the Hurlingham Polo Association's official rules. He also brought mallets and balls. The first American polo game took place at a riding academy in New York City. When spring came, they moved the games to a field in Westchester County, New York, and then to Newport, Rhode Island. It wasn't long before the game was being played all over the country.

WHO PLAYS POLO

Polo has always been associated with nobility and with wealthy people. In ancient Persia, it was played by kings, queens, and princes.

WHAT'S IN A NAME?

The name *polo* is thought to have come from the Tibetan word *pholo*, which means ball or ballgame. It might also have come from the Tibetan word *pulu,* which is a type of willow tree used to make the ball.

This gave it the nickname "the sport of kings." Even when it spread to England and to the United States, it was still seen as a game for the middle and upper classes. This is probably because playing polo involves having at least two horses for each game. This makes polo an expensive hobby. Today polo is played in approximately 80 different countries around the world. It lost some of its popularity when armies stopped using horse cavalry and switched to trucks and tanks. But today it still has many enthusiastic players and fans.

An American and a British polo team play each other in New York in 1930.

3

THE RULES OF THE GAME

In polo, the object of the game is to get the ball through the other team's goal. A player hits a small plastic or air-filled ball with a long-handled wooden mallet. The mallet looks like a longer version of a croquet mallet. Players can be male or female. They must play right-handed to avoid crashing into other players when going after the ball. The hardest part of the game is that the ball must be hit from the back of a moving horse. The rider must be able to follow and hit the ball while he or she controls the horse at the same time.

While polo players must hold mallets in their right hands, they can reach over their horses and hit on the left side.

Indoor arenas are 300 feet (91 m) long by 150 feet (46 m) wide. A football field is 360 feet (110 m) long and 160 feet (49 m) wide.

AT A GAME

The polo field, called the pitch, is the largest field used in any organized sport. It is almost 10 acres (4.1 ha) in size. Outdoor fields are 300 yards (274 m) long by

160 yards (146 m) wide. The goal posts on each end are 8 yards (7.3 m) apart. Polo is also played in indoor stadiums. Because polo is played both indoors and outdoors, there is no polo season. It is played year-round.

The game lasts approximately two hours. It is divided into periods called chukkers. Each chukker is 7 minutes and 30 seconds long. There is a break of three minutes between chukkers, and the player usually changes horses at this time. This keeps horses fresh for the game. At high levels, players might have a new horse for each chukker. Halftime is a five-minute break. At this point, the spectators are allowed onto the pitch, where they stamp down the divots in the grass that have been churned up by the horses' hooves.

OTHER WAYS TO PLAY POLO

Some very different forms of polo have developed over the years. In Saint Moritz, Switzerland, an annual polo tournament is played in the snow. In some parts of the world, polo is played on elephants or yaks instead of horses. Polo can also be played using bicycles, Segways, or even canoes.

The number of players varies depending on where the game is being played. On an open field outside, teams consist of four players on horseback. Indoor arenas are smaller than outdoor arenas. In an indoor arena, there are just three players per side. Each player has a specific purpose. Number One is the most offensive player, moving the ball toward the other team's goal. Number Two is also an offensive player, passing the ball to Number One for scoring. Number Three is usually a powerful hitter who passes the ball to the first two players. Number Three will also play defense and is usually the best player on the team. Number Four is mostly a defensive player. He or she can move anywhere on the field but usually tries to prevent the other team from scoring so his or her teammates can concentrate on scoring. There is no dedicated goalie in polo. After each goal is scored, or at halftime if there have been no goals, the teams switch ends of the field. A goal is worth one point.

Two umpires on horseback officiate the game on the field. A referee sits in the stands and acts as the decision-maker if the umpires disagree. A goal judge behind each goal waves a flag every time a goal is made. A timekeeper tracks the match's time and signals the end of each chukker. The scorekeeper tracks goals and fouls.

PLAYING THE GAME

The throw-in starts the game. The teams face each other. The umpire rolls a ball between the teams, and they try to hit the ball. When one rider is directing the ball, another can ride alongside and try to bump his or her pony into the other rider's mount. This is called a ride off. This can push the other rider away from the ball, and the rider can then hit the ball. However, if a rider is hitting a ball, another rider cannot pass in front of the direction the ball is headed if there is a slight risk of the ponies hitting each other. Doing this leads to a penalty where the game stops. After the penalty, gameplay begins a distance away from the goal that is determined

One umpire watches each side of the field.

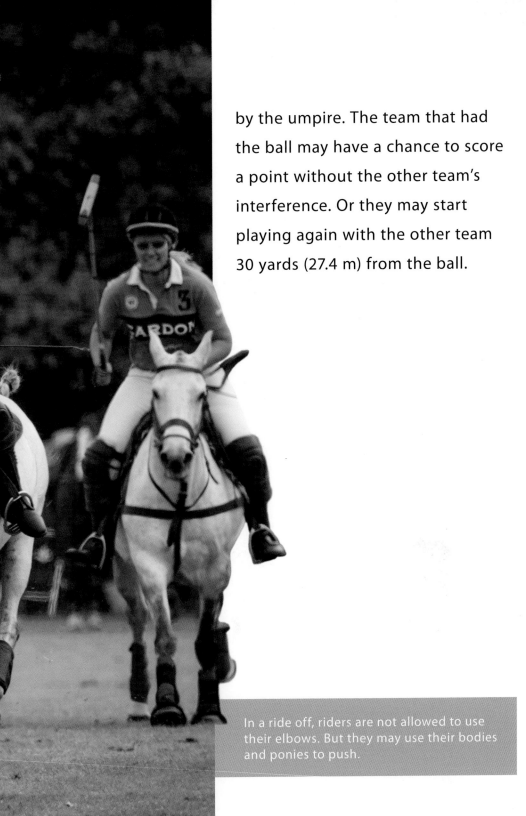

by the umpire. The team that had the ball may have a chance to score a point without the other team's interference. Or they may start playing again with the other team 30 yards (27.4 m) from the ball.

In a ride off, riders are not allowed to use their elbows. But they may use their bodies and ponies to push.

THE PLAYERS: HORSE AND RIDER

Polo is a fast sport. Riders need to be able to hit the ball while galloping at up to 35 miles per hour (56 km/h). This requires a good relationship between horse and rider. Riders also need to keep an eye on the rest of the field. They have to avoid running into other horses, and they need to keep track of their teammates.

Riders also need proper gear. They wear knee-high riding boots and kneepads. They wear helmets, which may have face guards to protect their faces from the mallets. Riders may use spurs or a whip to help give cues to the

The speed of polo means players must remain focused and aware of the other players on the field.

pony. But the most important players in a polo game aren't human.

POLO PONIES

The success of a polo team depends on its horses. Even though they are traditionally called polo ponies, they are actually full-sized horses. And just like a race car driver can't win a race without a good, fast car, the best polo player in the world isn't going to win unless he or she has an excellent horse.

A ROYAL FAMILY TRADITION

Britain's royal family has always been active in sports that involve horses. The male members of the British royal family are devoted polo players. King Edward VIII played in many polo tournaments in India and England. Prince Charles played polo for more than 40 years, and his sons, Prince William and Prince Harry, also play. Prince Harry even considered professional polo as a career before he went into the armed forces.

Because polo requires speed, a single horse would get too tired playing an entire match. Most polo players have at least two or three ponies and often more.

Even at the highest levels, riders may use their best ponies more than once in a game.

29

For a polo match with six chukkers, a team may have 50 horses combined!

PONIES OF CHOICE

The original polo ponies were the Manipuri ponies from India. But as the game evolved, the players needed faster horses. They began using Thoroughbred horses or Thoroughbreds mixed with Criollo or American quarter horses, sometimes with the same traits as racehorses. Thoroughbreds are larger with stronger muscles, and they can run faster. The average polo pony is between 15 and 16 hands tall. A hand is the measurement used to tell a horse's height. One hand is 4 inches (10.2 cm), and horses are measured from their withers, or the ridge between their shoulder blades, to the ground. Polo ponies used to be only 13 to 14 hands tall, which is why they were called ponies. Most polo ponies are mares. Some people believe they are more intelligent.

Thoroughbreds are popular polo ponies because of their speed.

IMPORTANT SKILLS

Polo ponies start training when they are approximately three years old. They become calm, alert, and obedient. They learn to be fast and smooth and to make quick, precise movements. They must understand the cues given by their rider through neck reining as well as through the rider's seat and legs. They have to get used to yelling players and being bumped by other horses. They must also ignore the cheering crowds and movement taking place in the stands. Some polo ponies are competitive like their riders. They will even try to keep other ponies from "stealing" the ball from them. Once a polo pony is fully trained, it can play until it is 18 to 20 years old.

PONY EQUIPMENT

A polo pony needs certain preparations before it can get out on the field. Its mane is shaved so it doesn't get in the rider's face. Its tail is taped up so the mallets don't get tangled in it. A pony also needs special tack, or riding gear. They have leg wraps and boots to protect their legs.

Polo ponies must be trained to be focused even around other horses.

They often have studs on their shoes. These are metal pieces that screw into the shoe and give the pony grip as it runs. Some riders use a gag bit. This steers the horse by putting pressure on the corners of its lips. Others use a Pelham bit. This can put pressure either on the corners of the pony's lips or on its lower jawbone. Both bits allow riders to give horses subtle cues. Two sets of reins attach to the bit.

A breastplate attaches to the saddle. It runs around the horse's chest to keep the saddle from slipping. A martingale runs from the bridle's noseband to the breastplate. This keeps the pony from hitting the rider with its head. All of this tack keeps pony and rider safe during a game.

The polo pony is the polo player's most important piece of equipment. Winning or losing a match depends largely on how smart the pony is. Polo experts say that even average riders can play far above their actual skill level if they have a brilliant horse.

GEAR

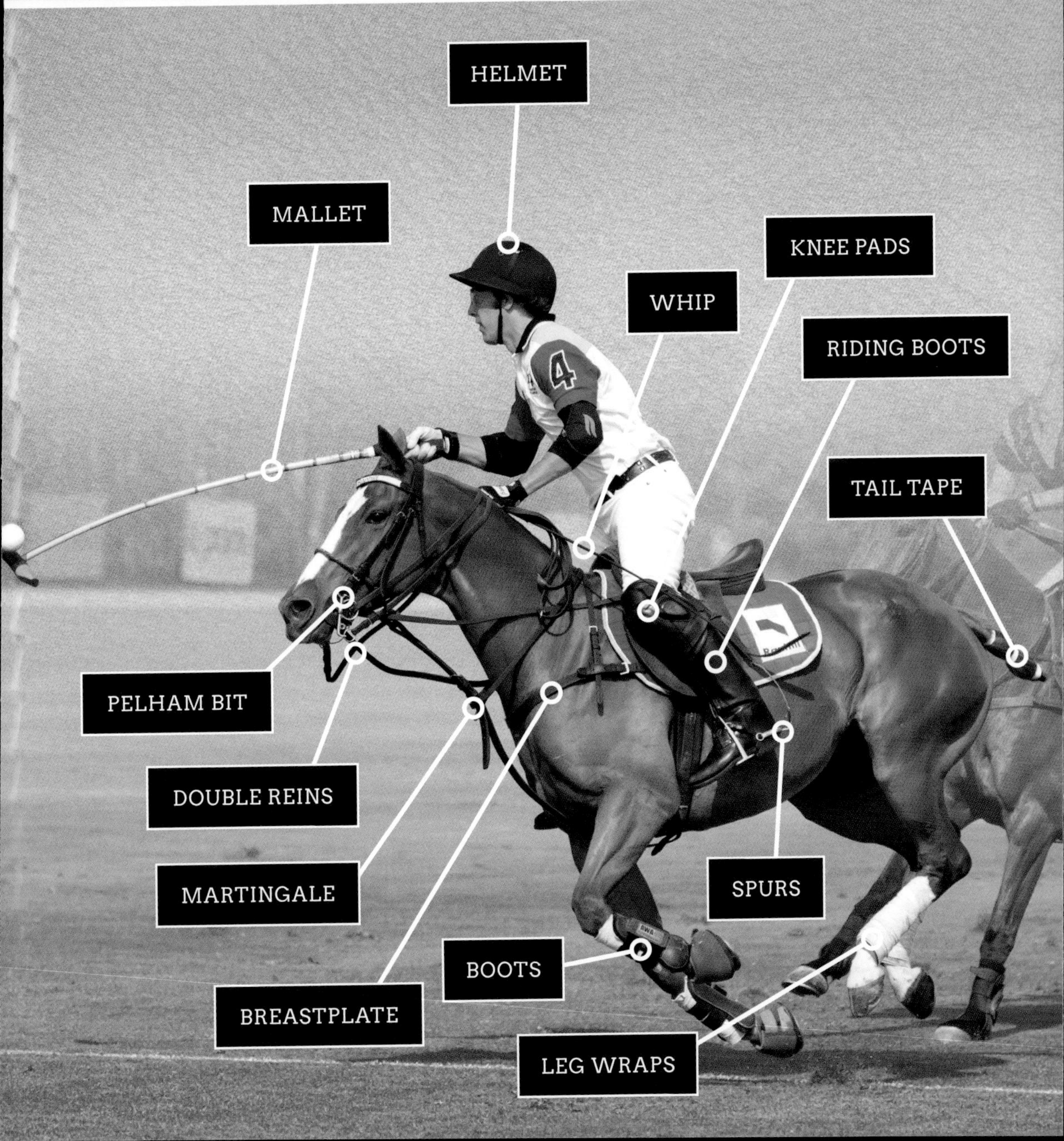

HELMET

MALLET

KNEE PADS

WHIP

RIDING BOOTS

TAIL TAPE

PELHAM BIT

DOUBLE REINS

MARTINGALE

SPURS

BOOTS

BREASTPLATE

LEG WRAPS

5

PLAYING POLO AROUND THE WORLD

Polo is a worldwide sport with international tournaments as well as local and national clubs and teams. One early international polo tournament took place in 821 CE, when Chinese ambassadors in Japan are said to have played against the Japanese emperor's team. Since then, polo's popularity has had its ups and downs, but there are plenty of players and spectators who love the game.

Some polo games are played in Dubai, United Arab Emirates.

POLO AROUND THE WORLD

The sport of polo takes place on a local level in organized polo clubs. The first club in the United States was the Westchester Polo Club, formed in New York in 1876. In 1890 the United States Polo Association was created. By 1900 there were 23 polo clubs, and today there are 275 clubs across the United States with more than 4,500 players. At first, polo was a sport only for the rich. But soon players with less money began to emerge, and wealthy teams welcomed these professional players. Today there are many professional polo players who make their living playing polo. They also earn money by training and selling

Polo matches are held at clubs around the United States, including at Sarasota Polo Club in Florida.

England won the 2013 Westchester Cup 12–11.

ponies, teaching others to play, and managing polo clubs. Polo clubs started attracting corporate sponsors in the 1970s.

Polo is an international sport with teams from all over the world competing against each other. The first

tournament in the United States took place against a British team in 1886. The prize was a silver trophy called the Westchester Cup. The British team won. Since then, the British team has won six times and the Americans 11. The Cup of the Americas (*Copa de las Americas*) is awarded to the winner of a tournament between the United States and Argentina. The United States and Mexico compete for the Camacho Cup. The Federation of International Polo now sponsors tournaments in the United States, China, Chile, Canada, Azerbaijan, and Germany.

WOMEN IN POLO

Polo is sometimes thought of as a man's game, but there are many women playing polo, too. When women first began to play polo in the 1950s, they had to disguise themselves. Sue Sally Hale, a pioneer female polo player, would dress like a man and even wear a fake mustache so that she could play. Her daughter, Sunny Hale, became

Some polo teams are made entirely of women.

the first woman to compete on a winning team during the 2000 US Open polo tournament. Women weren't allowed to join the US Polo Association until the 1970s, but today they make up approximately 40 percent of the members. Women can play alongside men in polo. But there are also women's polo leagues. Women's polo is popular in clubs as well as at high schools and colleges. In 2016, two women-led teams competed in the US Polo Association East Coast Open, one of the most prestigious polo tournaments in the United States.

OLYMPIC POLO

Polo was played during the Summer Olympic Games in 1900, 1908, 1920, 1924, and 1936. It was discontinued in part because few countries could send a polo team to the games. There were also difficulties in getting so many polo ponies to other countries. However, the Federation of International Polo has applied to have polo included in the 2020 Olympic Games in Tokyo.

A GROWING SPORT

Many people around the world enjoy playing and watching polo. Since World War II, the game's popularity has been growing. It's partly because the game requires both a capable player and a well-trained, skilled horse. Not only do players have to work well with their teammates, but they also need to have a very close relationship with their polo ponies. In today's world of sports, polo is gaining new players and fans. It is still one of the most exciting sports to play.

Polo riders can bond with their horses through training and spending time with them.

GLOSSARY

BIT
The mouthpiece of a horse's bridle, usually made of metal.

CAVALRY
A division of the military formerly involving soldiers on horseback.

DEFENSE
The player in a game who tries to keep the other team from scoring.

DIVOT
A piece of soil or turf that is dislodged by a hoof or mallet during a game.

GALLOP
A fast four-beat run.

MALLET
A long-handled wooden stick with a head like a hammer.

MARE
A female horse.

NOBILITY
Aristocrats and other people from a high social level.

OFFENSIVE
Having to do with the player who has the ball and is trying to score a goal.

PLANTATION
A large estate where crops such as sugar, tobacco, and tea are grown.

SPECTATOR
A person who watches a game, a show, or another event.

STAMINA
A horse's ability to do work without tiring.

TOURNAMENT
A series of contests between many teams who are competing for an overall prize.

UMPIRE
The official in a game who enforces the rules and makes decisions.

ONLINE RESOURCES

Booklinks
NONFICTION NETWORK
FREE! ONLINE NONFICTION RESOURCES

To learn more about horse polo, visit **abdobooklinks.com**. These links are routinely monitored and updated to provide the most current information available.

MORE INFORMATION

BOOKS

Harris, Susan E. *The United States Pony Club Manual of Horsemanship: Basics for Beginners/D Level*. Hoboken, NJ: Wiley, 2012.

Sanderson, Whitney. *Intro to Horse Racing*. Minneapolis, MN: Abdo, 2018.

Wilsdon, Christina. *For Horse-Crazy Girls Only: Everything You Want to Know About Horses*. New York: Feiwel & Friends, 2010.

INDEX

Bennett, James Gordon, 13

chukkers, 20, 21, 30
clubs, 7, 12, 36, 38, 40, 44

Federation of International Polo, 42, 44

gear, 26, 33, 35
goal, 4, 6–7, 8, 16, 21, 22

Hale, Sue Sally, 42
Hale, Sunny, 42
halftime, 7, 20, 21

mallets, 4, 7, 13, 16, 26, 33, 34
Manipuri ponies, 30

Olympics, 44

penalty, 22
pitch, 18, 20
players, 4, 6–7, 8, 10, 16, 20–21, 29, 30, 34, 38, 42, 44–45
Polo Association, US, 38, 44
polo ponies, 22, 29–30, 33–34, 38

referees, 21
ride off, 22

spectators, 7–8, 20, 36

tack, 33–34
Thoroughbred horses, 30
throw-in, 22
tournament, 12, 20, 29, 36, 41–42, 44,
training, 8, 10, 12, 33, 38

umpires, 21–22, 25

Westchester Polo Club, 38

ABOUT THE AUTHOR

Marcia Amidon Lusted has written more than 150 books and 600 magazine articles for young readers. She is also an editor and a musician. She grew up with horses.